AUDIO
ACCESS
INCLUDED

PLAYBACK+
peed • Pitch • Balance • Loop

ALTO SAX

A NEW MUSICAL
WICKED

T0082062

To access audio visit:
www.halleonard.com/mylibrary
Enter Code
4920-2933-1117-1045

ISBN: 978-1-4234-4968-3

7777 W. BLUEMOUND RD. P.O. BOX 13819 MILWAUKEE, WI 53213

Visit Hal Leonard Online at
www.halleonard.com

AS LONG AS YOU'RE MINE

ALTO SAX

Music and Lyrics by
STEPHEN SCHWARTZ

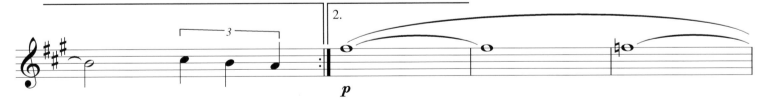

DANCING THROUGH LIFE

ALTO SAX

Words and Music by
STEPHEN SCHWARTZ

DEFYING GRAVITY

ALTO SAX

Words and Music by
STEPHEN SCHWARTZ

Allegro, as before

Slower

FOR GOOD

ALTO SAX

Words and Music by
STEPHEN SCHWARTZ

Più mosso

I COULDN'T BE HAPPIER

ALTO SAX

Words and Music by
STEPHEN SCHWARTZ

I'M NOT THAT GIRL

ALTO SAX

Words and Music by
STEPHEN SCHWARTZ

Simple and steady

NO GOOD DEED

ALTO SAX

Words and Music by
STEPHEN SCHWARTZ

ONE SHORT DAY

ALTO SAX

Music and Lyrics by
STEPHEN SCHWARTZ

15

Allegro

poco a poco rit.

Slower **Tenderly**

a tempo

POPULAR

Words and Music by
STEPHEN SCHWARTZ

ALTO SAX

WHAT IS THIS FEELING?

Words and Music by
STEPHEN SCHWARTZ

ALTO SAX

To Coda

CODA

D.S. al Coda

THE WIZARD AND I

Words and Music by
STEPHEN SCHWARTZ

ALTO SAX

dim. e rit.

Freely

a tempo

mf

Dreamily

mp

Freely

rall.   *f a tempo*

Broadly

rall.   *ff*   *accel.*

poco a poco accel.

Bright, triumphant

f

cresc.   *molto rall.*

ff a tempo

WONDERFUL

ALTO SAX

Music and Lyrics by
STEPHEN SCHWARTZ

NO ONE MOURNS THE WICKED

ALTO SAX

Words and Music by
STEPHEN SCHWARTZ